SEO FOR BL(

C000173857

A Beginner's Guide to Using SEO for Your Blog and Make Money Online

BOOK DESCRIPTION

Blogging is no doubt the most widely used way of publishing information on the internet. There are millions of blogs running on the internet. Moreover, each of the major websites have a blog section where quick updates can be made and users login to interact with authors and publishers regarding information in the published content.

This book starts by introducing blogging in its first section so that the reader gets acquainted with the basics before delving further into the deeper details of blogging for SEO. Choosing a blog niche for your entire blog, and topic niche for your particular post is the crucial first step to optimizing your blog for SEO. The second Section dwells on how you can go about choosing the most appropriate blog niche and blog topic.

Due to popularity of blogging, various platforms have come about to make it so easy for someone to create own blog. This book does an in-depth user-based analysis of the various blogging platforms and recommends the best platform that you can use to maximize gains of your blogging endeavor.

Once you have installed your blogging platform, the next logical step is to carry out Search Engine Optimization (SEO) of every facet of it so that surfers who search for its content can easily find it available. There is a complete section that shows you how to optimize your website for SEO.

Each blog post is an independent unit, only that it is contained within your blog website. Each is ranked independently by search engines. Thus, optimizing the website alone is not enough. It is imperative that you also optimize each blog post for maximum impact. This book has a section specifically dedicated to showing you skills, techniques and tools required for you to optimize your blog post. In this regard, there are two very important tools that have been discussed in detail – SEO Quake and SEO Yoast which enhance the optimization of your blog post. In addition there, several other tools that have been recommended for your further exploration.

Generating traffic to your blog is no mean task. It needs marshaled effort on your side. SEO alone, though critical, is not sufficient. You need to employ other ways which can complement SEO to drive traffic to your blog. These other ways to generate traffic to your blog are amply discussed in detail in a section of their own.

Every effort needs reward. You need to be rewarded for your blogging endeavor so as to cover your cost of blogging and even earn enough to make a living out of blogging. This is absolutely possible. This guide, Blogging for SEO, introduces and explores in detail the best 5 ways to monetize your blog. Getting incomes that can enable you to earn off your blogging endeavor requires not just effort but also smartness and creativity. Yes, you need to automate your income so that you continue earning even when you are in deep sleep or at the beach. The last section of this book provides you with sufficient ways and means by which you can automate your income so that you can continue gaining from its multiplier effect – day and night, 24/7, all year round.

Enjoy reading!

ABOUT THE AUTHOR

George Pain is an entrepreneur, author and business consultant. He specializes in setting up online businesses from scratch, investment income strategies and global mobility solutions. He has built several businesses from the ground up, and is excited to share his knowledge with readers.

DISCLAIMER

CONTENTS

INTRODUCTION

The blogging world has expanded in leaps and bounds. It has transcended geographical boundaries and created a new boundless community of dedicated bloggers. It has created new ways of people sharing knowledge and information. New standards have come about to enhance how this information is found and availed. Search Engine Optimization has not only become a new standard but a new profession. More importantly, it has become a new way of earning a living.

This book dwells into the depth of SEO Blogging, not necessarily a new but a unique, extremely dynamic and ever changing landscape in the blogosphere. This is to enable you to see the beauty of the landscape, cover acreages and confront new horizons that continue to manifest in each and every rising moment.

The blogosphere awaits you. It needs your citizenship. You can make immense contributions to this new world. Much more, you can discover new ways of earning a living doing what you love doing most – providing knowledge and information - about your passion, skills, talents and new discoveries.

Welcome to blogosphere! This book is your ticket to this ever-fresh world.

Thank you.

WHAT IS BLOGGING?

Blogging is the habit of posting content to a blog. This content is mostly in the form of articles which are commonly referred to as posts.

What is a blog?

A blog is a personal website where one posts content that he/she would like to publish.

Why do blogging?

There are as many different reasons for blogging as there are different personalities. Each person has his or her unique personality. However, the following are the main reasons as to why people do blogging;

1. Publish information – This is the core reason as to why people blog. Every piece of content that is posted to a blog is for purposes of it being published or simply made public.

2. Express one's passion – Blogging started off as a means for people to express and share their passion. People posted

articles in areas that they are passionate about, be it religious, political, social, relationships, among others.

3. Sharing one's skills, hobbies and talents - Most of the do-it-yourself blogs arose out of the need for people to share skills, hobbies and talents. Blogging is one of the best ways to connect with like-minded people as they read your mind and ideas as expressed through your blog.

4. Connect with like-minded people – Humans are social beings. They would naturally want to find opportunities to connect with others, especially those who are like-minded so that they can share ideas.

5. Campaigning for a cause – Blogs are a good way to campaign for a cause. Some of these causes include charity for the needy and destitute, campaign for the protection of the environment, campaign to force government to act in the interest of its citizens, campaign against crime and social ills, etc.

6. Promote products and services – Blogs have become a popular way for people, especially solopreneurs, to promote their products and services.

7. Make money – Making money online has increasingly become a way of earning a living for many. Blog monetization has become a popular way of making money online.

Why a blog?

A blog presents so many advantages over an ordinary website. Advantages of a blog over other kinds of websites include;

- You can easily manage and manipulate content

- You don't need to have advanced programming skills to install, run and manage it

- Most CMS, are by default, structurally SEO friendly

- You can change content without necessarily changing the structure of your website

Why is blogging so popular?

The popularity of blogging has continued to increase over time and doesn't show any signs of decline in the near future.

The following are some of the reasons that make blogging so popular;

- Prioritization by search engines – Search engines are configured to give preference to new content. Since a blog gets frequent post updates, it is perpetually renewed thus making it SEO-friendly and thus ranks relatively higher than ordinary websites in similar niche.

- Keeping connections live – Due to frequent updates; blogs get loyal following by those who anticipate some new posts. This helps to build a loyal following that stays lively interconnected.

- A great marketing tool – Blogging allows marketers to entertain prospects thus helping to build trust and rapport with them as potential leads.

- It is a great publicity tool – Business entrepreneurs find blogging as a great way of updating clients on the latest information. This information could be about a new product, new product features, new deal, new offer, etc.

Why passion and commitment is important to your blogging endeavor

Blogging is not like engaging in a sprint that you expect to finish up in a short while. Blogging is a marathon. You have to be persistent in your steps for long. Passion becomes your stamina and commitment your endurance.

The following are reasons why passion and commitment are important;

- **Blogging is time intensive** – For your blog to rank high in SEO and attract your desired audience, you have to keep on updating it with fresh content. It is this habit of always updating your blog that builds a loyal following that keep flocking your blog in anticipation of new content.

- **Blogging is a creative endeavor** – You need to keep on generating new ideas. You have to creatively capture and captivate your audience's imagination in order to eschew the traps of boredom and monotony that would naturally turn repulsive to them. In this endeavor, you should be able to decipher audience needs by carefully digesting their comments for telling signals of what they expect from you.

- **Blogging rewards build up over time** – While in some extraordinary cases you may succeed in climbing up so fast, in most ordinary cases, blogging takes time to build up rewards. It is a long-term endeavor. The good thing is that rewards can also last in the long-run if you keep up momentum.

Key blogging terminology

- Blog (noun) – a personal web

- Blog (verb) – to start a blog. To maintain a blog.

- Blog post – a piece of article posted onto a blog

- Blogging – the habitual act of posting content to and maintaining a blog

- Blogger – a person who engages in the act of blogging

- Blogosphere – an online community of bloggers

HOW TO CHOOSE A BLOG TOPIC AND NICHE

It goes without saying that blogs which attract a huge loyal following are those blogs that are niche-specific. Blog following honors the old adage that 'a jerk of all trades is a master of none'. If you are a blogger that writes about every other thing, you are easily going to expose your underbelly as a mediocre blogger. This is so because you cannot be an expert in all areas. Thus, you might be challenged in certain areas by those readers who are expert in those areas as probable errors, misrepresentation, misleading or shallow information due to your inadequacy of knowledge in the respective fields becomes apparent.

Hence, it is always good to pick up a particular niche depending on your target audience and your ultimate goal. This way, you keep yourself lean and fit with expert knowledge. You may not start off as a so-well-informed blogger in that particular niche, but, as practice makes perfect, you will hone your skills with time.

Many people who want to become bloggers always get held back by a cloudy mind characterized by so much information yet so obscure as to be precise. Refine your ideas first. Learn how to choose a niche. Learn how to choose a blog topic.

Steps to choosing your blog topic and niche

To be able to narrow down to your niche, you need to do the following so as to isolate the chaff from good;

1. Scribble down all that you think you can write on.

2. Itemize what you have scribbled down into more coherent topics.

3. Group these topics into categories based on their similarities.

4. Refine these categories based on your passion by removing from them all you think you can write on but don't feel passionate about.

5. Refine the categories further by selecting only what you think you are sufficiently knowledgeable in or you have the potential to gather sufficient knowledge on them.

6. Repeat steps (1) to (5) adding any new topic that comes to your mind that meets the mentioned criteria.

7. Rank these categories according your own order of priority based on your own balance between knowledge, passion, goal and target audience.

8. The category that ranks highest become your niche.

9. Rank topics within your niche according to your own order of priority based on your own balance between knowledge, passion, goal and target audience.

10. Create optimized titles based on your ranking (See the section titled "How to Optimize Each Blog Post" for details on how to optimize your title).

11. You can start creating optimized articles one-by-one based on your ranking in (9) and their respective titles in (10) above (See the section titled "How to Optimize Each Blog Post" for details on how to optimize your blog content).

WHICH BLOGGING PLATFORM SHOULD I USE?

The core essence of any blogging platform is its Content Management System (CMS). A CMS is a system that helps you to manage your content. It includes creating, editing, publishing and saving content, among others manipulations. These CMS platforms are differentiated by the following factors;

- Programming language

- License type

- Hosting type

- Pricing

Programming language

There are many programming languages. Programming language is extremely important as it will determine how easily you can access professional help should you desire to tweak or customize some CMS features.

The following are the most popular programming languages for CMS (server-side);

- PHP

- C#

- Java

- Python

- Node.js

PHP is by far the most popular CMS programming language. As such, it is easy for you to learn or get professional help should you desire to tweak or customize your blog. Most popular blog platforms including WordPress, Joomla and Drupal are written in PHP.

The second most popular CMS programming language is C#. But it comes at a very distant second to PHP. Java and Python are less popular. Node.js is a new entrant that is growing in leaps and bounds and is likely to grab a big share in future as it continues to increase in popularity. It is more likely to rival PHP in the near future. For the time being (as of publishing this guide), there are very few host providers for Node.js, C# and Java.

License type

Coming close to programming language is the license type (which is dependent on the language used). There are basically two main types of licenses:

- Open source license – Open source license allows you free access to programming codes (source codes). This is extremely important when you want to tweak or customize your blog. PHP, Java, Python, Node.js are all open source programming languages.

- Proprietary license – Unlike open source license, proprietary license is associated with closed source programs. Being closed source means that you cannot access all or some parts of the source codes. Thus, it is hard to tweak or customize the platform as desired to suit your particular needs. C# is partially proprietary and partially open source. While you can access, tweak and customize some codes, backbone codes and the engine that drives them is inaccessible.

Hosting type

Hosting simply refers to providing server space for the blog to run and connecting to an address (domain URL) for it to be accessible on the internet.

Hosting type is determined by two critical factors;

- Server OS (Operating System) – There are two major types of Server OS – Windows and Linux. So far, Linux is the most popular server OS for internet. Over 80% of websites and blogs run on Linux server. This is majorly because Linux OS is free and open source while Windows OS is paid-for and proprietary.

- The hosting party – Hosting party simply refers to the person in charge of hosting your website or blog. There are two types of hosting parties; self-hosted and non-self-hosted. Self-hosted simply means you are responsible for hosting the blogging platform. Non-self-hosted simply means that the provider of the blogging platform hosts it on your behalf.

Pricing

There are two pricing options when it comes to blogging platforms;

- Free – A free blogging platform simply means you don't pay anything to acquire it.

- Paid-for (non-free) – Paid-for blogging platform simply means that you have to pay to acquire it.

Popular CMS

There are over 50 CMS in the market today. However, the most popular CMS are;

- WordPress

- Drupal

- Blogger

- Joomla

Recommended choice criteria

The best platform to choose should have the following key features;

- Programmed in a most widely used language – PHP is the most preferred as it is most popular and can be hosted on Linux server

- Linux hosted – Linux servers run over 80% of blogs and websites across the globe. You can easily find a host provider on Linux unlike Windows.

- Open source – PHP is the most popular open source language for blogging platforms. Node.js is competing for the second place.

- Self-hosted – Your content is your property, your investment and your wealth. You obviously need to own it! Self-hosting is the only guarantee that you own your content and thus can fully monetize it.

- Free! – Why pay when you can get it free? Surprisingly the best blogging platforms are free. WordPress, Joomla and Drupal are absolutely free.

Why self-hosted WordPress is the best CMS for you

There is no doubt that, if you consider your content as your most important asset, then, you would naturally want to self-host. Also, you would naturally desire to spend less cost on acquiring the CMS. This rules out blogger and other non-self-hosted CMS. It also rules out non-free CMS. In this case, there are very few candidates left to compete with self-hosted WordPress CMS. Such other competitors include Drupal, Joomla, among others.

However, WordPress stands out from the crowd due to the following reasons;

- It is less bulky.

- It is easy to use.

- It has a large community of users.

- It has the largest community of developers.

- It is so easy to install.

- There are plenty of plugins that can help you optimize SEO, monetize, automate income, and many others.

- There are plenty of themes to boost the 'look and feel' of your blog.

Most host providers can install WordPress for you at no extra cost. There are several specialized WordPress host providers that you can engage to help you out on this.

Steps to building your blog

The following are important steps that will guide you in building your blog;

1. Determine your type of blog

2. Choose a domain name

3. Register your domain

4. Open a host account

5. Install your blog CMS

6. Create blog content

7. Promote your blog (so as to build audience and generate traffic).

8. Monetize your blog

9. Automate your income

Choose a domain name

Choosing your domain name is extremely important for purposes of SEO and user scanning.

The following steps will help you choose the most appropriate domain for your blog;

1. Come up with a domain name that matches your niche
2. Match the domain name with seo keywords of your niche
3. Make the domain name as short as possible (without compromising on 1 & 2 above) – this is for easy scanning and memorization by readers
4. Choose non-limiting domain extension (e.g .com, .net, .org)
5. If domain you want is taken, slightly modify it without stripping it of core essence (1 & 2 above)

Register your domain name

Once you have a domain name, the next thing is to register your domain. The process of registering, though extremely simple (and largely automated), varies from one domain registrar to the other. In case of difficulties, you can always get assisted by your domain name registrar in the setup process.

The following are popular domain registrars where you can easily register your domain;

- Namecheap

- Godaddy

Namecheap is the most preferred of the two options. Godaddy used to be the best but it has descended due to its insistence of compliance with government policies that restrict internet freedom, more so, when it comes to protecting the anonymity and privacy of domain ownership.

Open a host account

Once you have registered your domain, the next step is to host your domain account. Hosting is simply providing a space for your web content and directing your domain address to it so that the web content can be available when people enter your domain address to access it.

There are thousands of hosting service providers. However, the following are the most known;

- Hostgator

- Bluehost

- Siteground

- Scalahosting

The process of hosting varies from one host provider to another. Nonetheless, most hosting providers would be willing to guide you in setting up your website at no extra cost.

Install your blog CMS

Once you have successfully registered your domain and it has fully propagated (that is, the domain name is recognized by servers across the world) you can go ahead and install your WordPress blog.

Most hosts, like the ones mentioned above, have CPanel. CPanel is simply a dashboard with tools and resources that enables you to manage and optimize your website. The most popular of these tools is known as <u>Softaculous</u>.

<u>Softaculous</u> is a tool that enables you to install your WordPress blog without complications. It is automated. All you need is to fill in the required details in a form provided by it. These details include;

- Your blog name

- Your blog email address

- The folder in which you intend to install your blog (just provide the name of the folder). The folder must not exist as Softaculous will automatically create it.

- The place on the server where you want the folder to be created (by default, within 'public html' otherwise known as public directory). By default, Softaculous installs WordPress in the public directory. Thus, if you want to install in the public directory, leave the place for directory blank.

Once you provide these key details plus some other basic details, you simply need to click on the 'Install' button for Softaculous to automatically install the blog for you. Within 30 seconds, your blog will be up and running. You will be provided a URL address to the blog site and URL to the admin where you will log in with your admin credentials (username and password) to continue customizing your blog and adding content.

Select a great theme

Softaculous has a wide variety of themes which you can select prior to installing your blog (prior to clicking the 'Install' button). For a start, select an appropriate theme among those provided by Softaculous. You can later on easily change them when you find a better one that suits your content and layout through the admin panel.

You can find ideas on theme sources and other relevant information on WordPress from WPexplorer. Themeforest is another great place to find WordPress themes.

Create your blog content

For information on creating your blog content, please see the section titled "How to Optimize Each Blog Post".

Promote your blog

For information on how to promote your blog, see the section titled 'Other Ways to Generate Traffic'.

Monetize your blog

- For information on how to monetize your blog, see section titled "How to Monetize Your Blog".

Automate your income

For more information on automating your income, please read section titled "Automate Your Income".

OPTIMIZE YOUR WEBSITE FOR SEO

SEO has probably become the most widely used word by internet experts and entrepreneurs. It spells magic to so many, yet, it is simply a well-kept algorithmic secret of those who help to serve us web pages – search engines. Nonetheless there are both general and specific guidelines and tips availed by Search Engine providers and SEO experts.

What is a search engine?

Well, a search engine is simply a suite of programs that helps us get content that we seek to find over the internet. The internet today is a network of hundreds of thousands of servers across the world serving content and resources to millions of computers and gadgets across the globe.

The most popular search engines today are Google, Bing, Yahoo, Ask, Baidoo, Yandex, among others.

What is SEO?

Search Engine Optimization (SEO) is the technique of strategically creating and positioning your website such that it becomes easily accessible and available to those who seek it.

A website in this regard goes beyond just its content. It also includes its source codes, its structure and its flow (navigation). It is common for people to focus on the content alone when they talk of SEO to the detriment these other factors which are also critical.

What is SEO content?

When it comes to content, its utility matters a lot. Utility in this case means its ability to satisfy the want of those who seek it. In this regard, utility of form, place and time become critical. The content must be in the right form, that is, of the right quality. It must be at the right place. That is, be deliverable to those who seek it. It must be available at the right time, that is, as fast as those who seek it need it.

To make sure that the content obeys these three key utilities, it has to be packaged in such a manner that it is highly portable for quick delivery. Search engines are like cranes that lift this content and delivers to the intended place – the SERP (Search Engine Result Page). The content that best-fits user's utility needs get ranked highest and the rest get ranked next to each other according to their degree of utility.

The user places a search query with certain keywords (whether knowingly or unknowingly) to the search engine (via the search panel/window) requesting to be served a certain content. These keywords become the guides of which points on the content package that the search engine hooks will be placed. A package that has the most points matching the keywords will quickly and firmly anchored and its description details recorded (indexed) in the SERP for the user to unveil (click on) for more details.

Thus, SEO content is that content that has points (keywords) matching those keywords in the user's search query as close as possible.

How does SEO work?

So far, we have seen how seo works content-wise. However this is just but one part of it. Still using our analogy of the crane, for the crane to be able to lift up a package, the points (eyelets or holes) into which its hooks will be anchored should firmly etched on the package holders/container.

First of all, this package has a container. Then it has ropes tied around the container. The ropes have eyelets strategically placed for the hooks to easily reach and anchor. The eyelets should be balanced such that the package doesn't tilt or fall over while being lifted up.

The container, in a web sense, is a web page or post (which has the content). The ropes are the navigations that link to that particular web page. The eyelets are actually the keywords which the search engine will hook on as mapped by the user's query.

Once the search engine find a package that best-fits the user instructions (keyword queries), it announces these findings by registering (indexing) them on the SERP ranked on the best-fit order as a feedback/response to the user. The user now has a choice of selecting an index that he/she feels has the description (meta description) that best represents intent of his/her search query. The user exercises this choice by clinking on the index link which leads him/her to the web page with the content.

Why do we need SEO?

Having understood how search engines work, it is obviously necessary to help them in their endeavor to serve users. Quality service is the key. Thus, to make users (surfers) have the best experience on the internet when searching for content, search engine optimization (seo) becomes important.

SEO is about quality service delivery by websites that satisfies users' wants by meeting their key utility needs – form, place and time.

What are SEO techniques?

Seo techniques are those techniques employed to optimize web package delivery to the intended users. As we have seen, there are four core areas of seo;

- The skeleton (structure)

- The muscles (navigation links)

- The flesh (content)

- The DNA (identifiers – e.g. tittles, meta tags, captions, image file names, keywords, etc)

Each of these four areas must be optimized. A strong skeleton, weak muscle is bad; Strong skeleton, lean flesh is emaciation; Heavy flesh, weak muscles is obesity; Heavy flesh weak skeleton is a disaster.

Well, a great form (balanced skeleton, muscles and flesh) that is unknown (that lacks identifiers) can't be of use (lacks utility). Thus, the best seo technique is a one that makes sure that each of these four core elements is optimized, they are in harmony and balances out.

Why are Keywords so important in SEO?

Keywords are the language of identifiers by search engines. These are the pointers used by the surfer to direct search engine hooks.

When the user places a search query, the user may or may not know the web page that he/she is looking for. It is just like going to a place where people are and ask "I am looking for George". You probably know who George is, or, probably not. The name 'George' is an identifier. What if that place was a meeting place of all people called 'George'? You will have to give much more description (identifiers). Maybe you could add family name to "George" e.g. "George Washington", "George Marshal", "George O'Connor", etc. Maybe you could add an official title identifier such a "Prof. George", "Eng. George", "Adv. George", "Arch. George", etc. You could further give an image identifier e.g. "George the brown tall guy", "George the black short guy", "George the limping one". You could as well give place identifier such as "George from Washington", "George from London", "George from Nairobi", etc. There are many more identifiers of George including character identifiers, occupation identifiers, and socio-cultural identifiers, among many others. All these help to distinguish one George from dozens of others in a place (and even millions of others on the internet).

What are the primary, secondary and long-tail keywords?

Taking our example of George, the word "George" is a primary keyword. When this keyword is modified by title and surname (e.g. "George Marshal", "Prof. George", etc) each of the modified keyword becomes secondary keyword. When you have a keyword that not only identifies but also describes the identity, then, that becomes a long-tail keyword. For example "George from Nairobi" is a long-tail keyword as it not only identifies "George" but also describes where "George" comes from (or, in essence, where to find him). Also "George the brown tall guy" is a long-tail keyword as it not only identifies George but also describes his physical attributes".

What is the difference between short-tail and long-tail keywords?

Quantitatively, short-tail keywords basically have two to three words. Qualitatively, they are not detailed enough to describe user's needs and benefits.

On the other hand, quantitatively, long-tail keywords have more than three keywords. Qualitatively, long-tail keywords describe the user's particular need or benefit.

For example;

- "SEO expert" is a short-tail keyword. This keyword doesn't describe a particular need or benefit.

- "How to become an SEO expert" is a long-tail keyword. This keyword describes a user's particular need of "becoming an SEO expert".

- "How to make money being an SEO expert" is also a long-tail keyword. This keyword describes a user's particular need of "making money doing SEO".

The most important dividing line between short-tail and long-tail keywords is not necessarily quantitative but largely qualitative. Just having many words jumbled up together without any identifiable need or benefit doesn't make it a long-tail keyword.

Why short-tail keyword is a "necessary" noise

In signal language, a signal or set of signals with confusing or non-perceptible information are known as noise. A search query is in fact an amalgam of electronic signals. A short-tail keyword in a search query will quickly populate the SERP and are more likely going to have so many SERPs. Why so? Simply because search engine is rather confused or hasn't perceived well the user's query.

Thus, to optimize on your SEO endeavor, it is important to limit the noise by using long-tail keywords.

Why long-tail keywords are essential for your SEO?

Long tail keywords, as illustrated above, help to isolate a particular entity from a crowd of others. They help the search engine to be more precise.

The following are important reasons as to why you should consider long-tail keywords in your SEO campaign;

- **They are less competitive** – Short-tail keywords are usually competitive, that is, there are many websites competing to deliver the package queried (demanded) by the user. Thus, the probability of your package being indexed on the SERP is minimal. On the other hand, long-tail keywords are less competitive. This is because they are more precise (relatively high-grade) and thus fewer websites are competing to deliver queried package.

- **They bring more serious leads** – Most ecommerce experts will tell you that long-tail keywords experience higher conversion rate than short-tail keywords. Why? This is simply because users who employ long-tail keywords in their search query are more serious and particular of exactly what they want – a particular need or benefit. Thus, they are more likely to respond positively to the package they are offered (e.g. reading, making a buy decision, consulting further, etc)

- **They have less bounce rates** – Bounce rates refers to the rate at which visitors leave without having been welcomed or having decided to take what is offered. It is like a stranger bumping into a wrong room or entering a wrong street and bounces back in haste. Due to long-tail keywords being more specific, bounce rates are low. A history of high bounce rates lowers your page ranking and visibility since the search engines get tired of keeping on presenting the wrong package to visitors. High bounce rate hurts your SEO.

- **They have relatively higher conversion rate** – Obviously, more serious leads (e.g. potential audience, potential buyers, etc) have higher conversion rate (yielding positive results e.g. sales, loyal audience, more following, etc) compared to less serious leads.

- **They have relatively higher yield** – It is always the intent of any rational person to get the most maximum benefit out of the least possible sacrifice. For example, if you have one web page that has 10,000 visitors per day, it is far less costly and much more beneficial compared to a host of 100 websites that yields the same number of visitors per day. On the other hand, having product page that has 500 visitors per day of which 80 of them makes a buy decision is far more beneficial than having a website with 5,000 visitors per day only for less than 10 of them to make a buy decision. The high number of visits is important (most probably due to use of short-tail keywords) but a higher yield is much more important (most probably due to use of long-tail keywords).

What is the difference between paid-search and organic search?

A paid search is a one where you pay a search engine provider to rank your page higher on the SERP. For example, if you search for something on Google, the SERP shows a tiny box with "ad" in it immediate before the title of the ranked web page.

An organic search is one that gets indexed naturally on SERP without the intervention of or monetary inducement to the search engine provider. It is in the organic search that keyword SEO becomes important.

What are SEO analytics?

SEO analytics refers to a set of tested outcomes based on given SEO criteria. The following are the most important criteria;

- Keywords

- Traffic flow (both inbound and outbound)

What are SEO tools?

SEO tools are those tools that aid you in your SEO endeavor. These tools fall into various categories. The following are the most important categories

- SEO Keyword suggestion tools – These tools helps to suggest keywords for your SEO campaign. Examples include Google Keyword Planner, Google Adsense, among others.

- SEO Analytics tools – these tools help you to analyze your web performance based on certain analysis criteria. Such tools include Google Analytics, Authority Labs, among others.

- SEO Diagnostic tools – These tools helps to diagnose problems that frustrates your website's SEO. <u>Google web master</u> has a suite of tools that helps you in this endeavor.

For more information on SEO tools, please read section titled "Other SEO Add-ins / Softwares to Use".

How do I monitor traffic on my website?

Monitoring your web traffic is extremely important in establishing the impact of your SEO campaign. This helps you to enhance that part of the campaign that gives maximum impact and correct any anomaly that make your campaign outcome constrained.

The following are the major tools that you can use to monitor traffic on your website;

<u>Google Analytics</u>

<u>Authority labs</u>

<u>Crazy Egg</u>

CHOOSING KEYWORDS FOR BLOG POSTS – SEO QUAKE

As we discussed in the previous section (SEO Optimize Website), it became abundantly clear that Keywords are an integral component of organic search and ranking on SERP.

In this section, we are going to dwell on choosing keywords for blog posts using one of the most incisive and popular SEO tools, SEO Quake.

To understand how choose keywords for blog posts using SEO Quake, it is important to first of all understand how to interpret its output by dissecting its SEO metrics.

SEO metrics by Quake

SEO metrics by Quake are simply criteria or parameters used to present output of a website's SEO performance analytics. These parameters are based on provisions by various data providers including Alexa, SEMrush, Pinterest, Facebook, among others. The following are the main types of SEO metrics that we are going to dwell on;

- Page metrics

- Domain metrics

- Backlink metrics

Page metrics

The following are the page metrics captured by SEO Quake that greatly aid in your keyword research endeavor;

- **Google Cache date** – this metric shows the last time Google created a cached version of the queried page.

- **Facebook Likes** – This indicates the aggregate likes that the queried page has garnered.

- **Google Plus One** –This metric shows the aggregate quantity of Google Plus One that the queried page has garnered.

- **LinkedIn share count** – This indicates the aggregate volume of LinkedIn shares that the page has garnered.

- **Pinterest Pin count** – This indicates the aggregate volume of pins that the page has collected.

- **Source** – This is the link to the page's source codes

Domain metrics

These are domain metrics relevant to the website URL of the page being displayed. These include;

- **SEMrush Rank** – This is unique SEMrush rating of a website's popularity based on organic traffic originating from Google's top 100 organic search results.

- **Google Index** – This refers to amount of indexed pages examined by Google for the domain being displayed. Bing Index, Baidoo Index, Yahoo Index are also similar to Google Index but by the respective providers.

- **Alexa Rank** - A ranking of the websites arrayed by ascending score, measured in millions. It is regarded as more sensitive than the indicator for PageRank. So, the lower your Alexa score, the better (i.e. 1 is better than 1000).

- **SEMrush SE Traffic** – This refers to the average volume of monthly traffic for the queried domain as estimated by SEMrush.

- **SEMrush SE Traffic Price** – this is a cost metric that gives a rough estimate of SEMrush's average cost per month that one would incur in bidding for a particular keyword queried. This is a rough monetary estimator of a keyword's competition. The lower the price the lesser the competition.

Backlinks metrics

Backlinks metrics provide data on the amount of external links leading to the page or domain being displayed.

- **Google Links** - how many backlinks Google has found providing a link to the queried page. SEMrush Links and Baidoo Link are same as Google Links except by their respective providers.

SEO Quake diagnostics

This gives various diagnostic indicators about the health of the respective web page in terms of optimization, traffic flows among others. The following are the most relevant indicators to your keyword research endeavor;

- **Google's Page Rank:** This is a measurement of general website strength and uses a logarithmic scale of 1 to 10. Like the earthquake scale, the difference between PR3 and PR4 is a lot greater than between PR1 and PR2. PR3 is a very respectable score; PR4 is more common for SEO companies. The highest PageRank is PR10.

- **Alexia traffic rank:** This number ranks websites from the best (1) to scores in the millions. It is more sensitive than the PageRank indicator.

- **Text/html ratio:** Measures the text compared to the coding on any given webpage. For search engine ranking, you need as much text as possible. Fifteen percent is adequate, but 50 percent or more is ideal.

- **Keyword density:** function can be used to analyze the words in the content you have created. Your keywords should ideally be included at the one percent level. Too much, and the search engines will think you are keyword stuffing and could penalize you. Too little, and your competitors will outrank you.

How to use the mentioned metrics in your Keyword research

Fundamentally, SEO Quake helps you to research competitors. Find the most highly ranked competitors within your niche and evaluate them on SEO Quake. In this regard;

1. Use domain metrics to rank your competitors so as to benchmark them as your standard.

2. Determine the keywords used by them that help to generate higher traffic

3. Determine how they have utilized those keywords (keyword density)

4. Use page metrics and diagnostics metrics as tools to evaluate your own web page performance once you have (1), (2) and (3) above as a gauge of your performance against competition.

To implement the specific keywords, use SEO Yoast (see next section titled "How to Optimize Each Blog Post")

HOW TO OPTIMIZE EACH BLOG POST?

The best thing with WordPress, it has a good number of SEO plugins. Yoast is by far the most popular and widely used WordPress SEO plugin. In this section we are going to focus our attention largely on how to optimize each of the blog posts using SEO Yoast.

When it comes to optimizing each blog post, the following are important things you must focus on;

- Ensure that your blog post is found and indexed by search engines;

- Make sure that your blog post is relevant to the subject matter, engaging to the audience , and helpful in meeting your audience needs

- Endeavor to make your blog post popular and authoritative, relative to competition.

The following are steps you need to take to optimize your blog post;

Step 1: Open A New Post Template

While in your Admin section, Click on Posts on the top left panel and select 'Add New'.

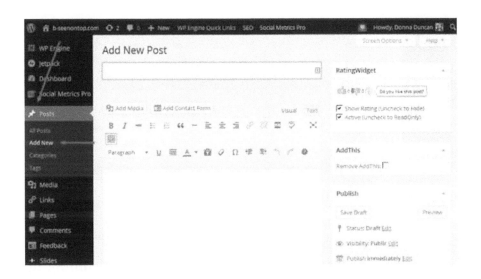

Step 2: Type in your body text

Skip entering the title of your post (see step 5 on how to enter title). You will optimize your title much later after optimizing your content. Instead, focus on what to enter in the body (identified by 'X').

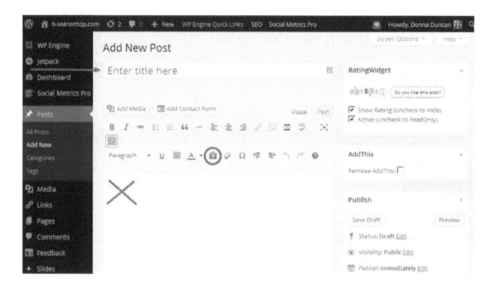

Step 3: Choose your Keywords

Choosing appropriate keyword is most important SEO task in this endeavor. The following steps will guide you in coming up with the most appropriate keywords;

1. Narrow the focus of your post;
2. Gather keyword options;
3. Assess the relevance, specificity, and search volume of options;
4. Use google planner to weigh in on potential traffic;
5. Assess uniqueness;
6. Pick secondary keyword phrases;
7. Enter your focus keyword into yoast plugin;

Step 3(a) Narrow The Focus of Your Post

Search Engines are always quick to rank higher those posts that are narrowly focused as they have higher potential of meeting user's particular search query.

To narrow the focus of your post, you must address the following key questions;

1. Is my post topic narrow and specific enough?

2. Does the topic accurately capture the core essence of my post?

Though you are not entering title by now, the topic will lead you into the scope of your content.

Step 3 (b) Gather Keyword Options so as to be able to determine focus keyword

The most important part of your keyword endeavor is to get the 'focus keyword' or simply 'primary keyword'. The focus keyword will enable you to get other keywords around it (that modifies it). These keywords are often known as 'secondary keywords'.

Since we are dealing with SEO optimization of a blog post, we have to derive a focus keyword that maps the likely user query in the search window. As indicated earlier, users search for "how to" as part of their intent either to satisfy a particular need or to derive a particular benefit. In our case, we can re-orient our topic to include "how to" in order to map to the most likely user query. We come up with "How to optimize a blog" as the most appropriate focus keyword in relation to our section topic.

To find secondary keywords, we enter this focus keyword into our Google search window. Why Google? Well, Google controls over 60% of internet search market. Users are more likely going to use it. Also, Google is basically the industry standard as far as Keywords are concerned. Also, Google has a range of sophisticated tools that can help us find these keywords. Of our current necessity is the tool called **Google Suggest**. Google suggest is a keyword tool that brings out search query suggestions based on user entry and to bring up common queries usually entered in relation to the user query. These common queries suggested by Google are the secondary keywords suggestions that we will have to look at.

Typing our focus keyword "How to optimize a blog" into the Google search window as shown in the figure below, we get quite a good number of suggestions appearing on the dropdown list below our entered query.

how to optimize a blog|
how to optimize a blog post for seo
how to optimize a blog post
how to optimize a blog for search engines
how to optimize a blog article
how to optimize a wordpress blog
how to optimize a blogger blog
how to optimize a tumblr blog
how to optimize blog for mobile
how to optimize blog post images
how to optimize your blog for search engines

Google Search   I'm Feeling Lucky

Step 3 (c) Assess Relevance

The keyword should be a best-fit reflection of your blog content. Thus, whether a particular keyword ranks highest or lowest on the suggest box is immaterial if it is irrelevant to your content. If you choose an irrelevant keyword, there will be high bounce rates (of users retreating for not finding appropriate content relevant to the chosen keyword). Most search engines (more so, Google) penalize your blog if it experiences high bounce rates by ranking it lower.

Step 3 (d) Assess Specificity

The given keyword must be specific to your blog content. This boosts your conversion rate. As discussed earlier, use long-tail keyword. You can derive this by utilizing suggestions provided by Google suggest tool as a guide.

Step 3 (e) Assess Search Volume

Search volume is an indicator of how much potential your chosen keyword has for generating traffic to your site. Use <u>Google Planner</u>. The following are results obtained by using <u>Google Planner</u> on our focus keyword "How to optimize a blog";

Step 3 (f) Use Google Planner to weigh in on potential traffic

The great thing about <u>Google Planner</u> is that it also provides volume metrics of suggested keywords which helps you create a long-tail keyword with high traffic volume potential. The following diagram shows our focus keyword "How to optimize a blog" with suggested keywords "how to optimize a blog post" and others.

Our focus keyword still ranks higher than the suggested keywords. Thus, we stick by it. However, if "how to optimize a blog post" or "how to optimize a WordPress blog" had ranked higher, then, we would have had to drop our focus keyword and chosen the one ranking higher as our new focus keyword (provided that it is relevant to the content).

Step 3(g) Enter Your Focus Keyword Phrase 'into Yoast '

With your focus keyword determined, scroll down to the box identified as 'WordPress SEO by Yoast" Click on it to open the template as appearing below.

Step 3 (h) Assess Uniqueness

The next step is to test the uniqueness of the focus keyword, that is, how unique is it relative to other blog posts on your website? It is important that you should not create internal competition between pages within your blog post as this will tire (and confuse) the search engine and thereby disadvantage you when it comes to competing with others web pages.

To make a quick analysis of the uniqueness of your focus keyword, create a quick draft using the focus keyword and then scroll down to the 'WordPress SEO by Yoast' window near the bottom of the post page. Click on the page analysis tab and scroll down to the second last bullet. If it reads "You've never used the focus keyword before, very good". That is an affirmation that your focus keyword is unique.

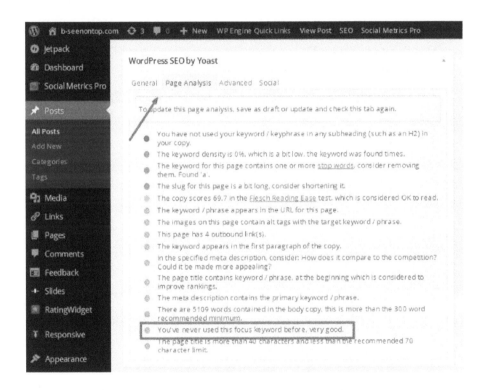

Step 3 (i) Choose Secondary Keyword Phrases

Google always considers related keywords when it comes to ranking. Thus, it is always prudent to get two to three related keywords (secondary keywords) to the focus (primary) keyword and use them sparingly within the content. This boosts your ranking probability.

The diagram below shows related keywords provided by Yoast based on entered focus keyword. As can be seen "How to optimize a blog post for seo" and "how to optimize blog post images" appears the most relevant and unique (differentiated from the focus keyword).

Step 3 (j) Put Your Focus Keyword Phrase Into The Plugin

Now, we finalize step 3 by entering our focus keyword into the plug-in.

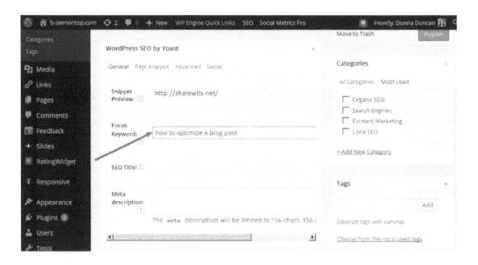

Step 4 Specify a SEO Title

The title has to be optimized for SEO. The following are the four criteria you need to ensure that your title is optimized;

- Select a title that accurately reflect your post content;

- Use your focus keyword phrase in the title;

- Let your title be compelling; and

- Let your title have between 40 and 55 characters. Nonetheless, they must not exceed 512 pixels in length. Any length beyond 512 pixels will be truncated by Google search engine.

Once the above criteria are met, put your SEO title into the Yoast Plug-in;

Step 5 Specify Your Post Title

Now, enter your post title in the space provided in the Post template as shown below;

Step 6: Specify Your Post Permalink

Permalink is your post's unique URL that searchers can click on to be directed to your post. This permalink is hyperlinked to your post title when it is indexed and ranked on SERP.

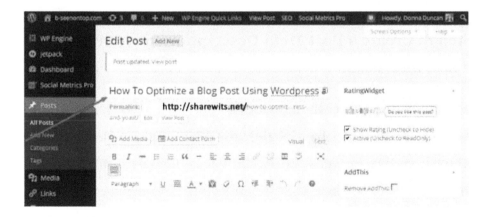

WordPress automatically enters permalink when you post the title. However, it is not always the best. Thus, you can check on it and modify it to ensure that it is appropriate.

Step 7: Incorporate Keywords Into Post Body Text

Now you can incorporate both your primary and secondary keywords into your body content. Let the primary keyword appear at least 3 times in the body – first paragraph, middle of the body and last paragraph. For 400 - 600 words, this is adequate to avoid keyword stuffing. For long posts, as a rule of thumb, you can put one keyword per every 200-300 words but don't overdo. Don't exceed 8-12 keywords however long the post is. Take advantage of secondary keywords instead (they must also obey keyword density, yet fewer than key focus keyword for it to remain 'focused').

Step 8: Create a Post Meta Description for your post and insert into Yoast

A meta description, though 'no longer' count for purposes of ranking (as claimed by Google), it still remains a best practice when it comes to websites. Nonetheless, Google admits that, if the content is unclear (has no relevant keywords), the search engine relies on meta description to 'tell' what the website is all about. That is a pointer enough not to discard it. A meta description is a short synopsis of your website etched within the head section of your blog.

Nonetheless, a meta description appears below the permalink in a page's index on SERP. This helps searchers to determine whether the indexed web page is what they are looking for or not.

Blog SEO for the Modern Marketer: How to Optimize Your ...
blog.hubspot.com/ /blog-seo-modern-marketer-optimize- ▼ HubSpot, Inc. ▼
Oct 9, 2013 · Once you have your list of blog posts, you'll want to make sure you've optimized the headlines. Keywords do best when they're at the front of ...

To optimize a meta description, the following are important;

- Incorporate focus keyword in your phrase

- Let your meta tag be relevant and convincing

- Use about 150 characters

- Avoid special characters, more so quotation marks

Once you have formulated your meta description, insert it into Yoast plug-in as shown below;

Step 9: Optimize your images

They say a picture speaks a thousand words. It is no secret that posts that have photos rank higher than those that don't have, other things remaining constant. A good photo attract user to read the content so as to know what the photo is all about.

To optimize your image;

- Set a featured image

- Insert Alt Tag

- Create a Caption

Set featured image

A featured image is important as it guides search engines which image (among several blog post images) to pick as the key image to associate with your blog post. This ensures uniformity of output when it comes to multiple search engines.

Set Featured Image box appears on the right sidebar of the Post template just immediately below the Tags. Once you click on the box it will lead you to the Album with a dialog box for you to select the right image and set other parameters including dimensions, cropping and thumbnails.

Insert Alt Tag

An Alt (Alternative) Tag is extremely important. It is a description that appears as an alternative to an image. An image may fail to appear for the following reasons;

- Slow loading due to poor internet

- Broken link

- Unsupported browser

- Server restrictions on the user's end

To optimize an Alt Tag;

- Make sure that it contains focus keyword

- Make sure that the tag is unique (never used for any other image within the blog)

- Make sure that it is as short as possible without compromising on clarity of information

- Make sure that it is relevant to the content

- Make sure that it has appropriate link (if you want user to be redirected to a certain page e.g. product page). Otherwise, Link to None.

Caption

A caption is a brief sentence or paragraph beneath a photo which helps to elaborate what the photo is all about. Though optional, it is good to have a caption. The caption should not be a conclusion or an alternative summary to the content but an explanatory leading statement that encourages reader to get more details in the content.

Step 10: Categorize and Tag Post

Categories are simply containers of related posts. Tags just like categories are unique classifiers that could run through various categories. For example, you can have several posts on SEO and thus put them under a category called 'seo'. On the other hand you can have several authors for your blog, each having written articles falling into various categories. A reader may be particularly interested in articles by a certain author. You can create a tag in the name of this author. Just like categories can appear in the post's URL, tags too can appear in the post's URL. Thus, the same post can have two URLs, one by category and another one by tag. This improves exposure and accessibility of a given post.

There are three types of tags that you will need to set for your post in Yoast (beside what entered and ticked in the right sidebar of the post's template);

- Canonical Tag

- Social Tag

- Noindex

Canonical Tag

This is a special tag that identifies your content as unique and original so that should there be a duplicate post, you won't be penalized by search engines as your post will be deemed the original one. Make it a habit of tagging each of your post as canonical so that you don't get penalized while the one who plagiarizes you gets bonus from your sacrifice.

Under canonical URL, leave it blank so that your web's URL will be entered automatically. However, if your content is a repost with permission from an external blog, put the URL linking to that particular post in the external blog as Canonical URL. This is, in essence, giving due credit to the owner of the blog.

Social Tags

Yoast has provision for social tags. These are simply tags describing what you would like to be posted about your blog post when shared on social media such as Facebook, Twitter, G+, LinkedIn, Facebook, etc.

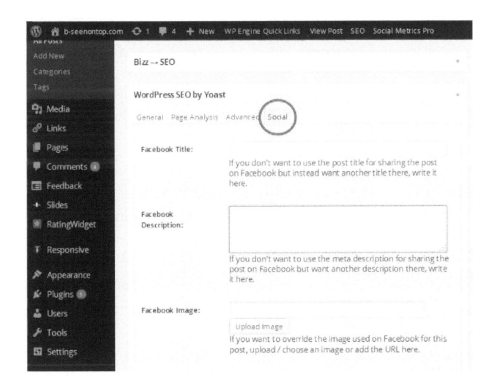

Noindex

Noindex is a tag that informs search engine, such as Google, not to index your blog. This is so important when your post doesn't meet Google ranking criteria and you don't want to be penalized for that.

The following describes content (thin content) that requires Noindex;

- Unoriginal content

- Keyword-stuffed content

- Auto-generated content

- Irrelevant content

- Undesirably short content (less than 300 words)

There could be reasons as to why you need to put thin content. Simply make sure that you don't get penalized by search engines by simply using Noindex.

Step 11: Specify The Post Author

Either below the body of the blog post (prior to posting) or under 'quick edit' after posting, you can set the author's name. Just check for 'Add Author' and insert the author's name. This is important, especially if your blog has multiple authors. There are those leaders who easily get hooked to an author's particular writing style. This helps them follow that particular author.

Step 12: Final Confirmation

To confirm that your page is optimized for SEO, go back to Yoast plug-in window and check whether your post has been given green to publish by confirming that the five indicators just below 'Focus Keywords' are all green;

If they are all green, you can comfortably publish your post. However, you must not overlook other quality factors that are not within Yoast's domain such as proper grammar, relevant content, logic flow, succulence, etc.

OTHER SEO ADD-INS / SOFTWARES TO USE

What makes WordPress popular as a CMS is the huge volume of Add-Ins (Plugins) due to a large active community of developers. There is virtually nothing extra that you will need to hire a developer for a blog in Wordpress. In case you don't find the right plug-in, there are several independent software that you can utilize to achieve your intended objectives.

In this section we listed appropriate Plugins and software that you can utilize in your endeavor to optimize your blog. The description for each Plug-in is beyond the scope of this book. Each Plug-in is hyperlinked so that you can click on it to be directed to appropriate Plug-in website where you can get further details on how to install and use it.

We have divided these plugins and software into the following broad categories;

- Content curation and management

- Content SEO

- Engagement, Publicity and Promotion

- Page loading efficiency

- Administrative

- Suites (a special mention of Jetpack)

Content management and curation apps/plugins

- Topic selection - Google Trends, BuzzSumo, SEMrush

- Content curator- Full Text RSS, MyCurator, WP RSS Aggregator, WP eMatico

- Anti-plagiarism – Copyscape, Plagscan

- Editorial Assistant by Zemanta

- Posts by Tag

- Related Posts by Zemanta

- Directories – Business Directory plug-in, Simple Link Directory plug-in,

- Forum boards - Quora, Warrior forum

- Videos - Youtube

- Landing page creation tools - <u>Ubounce</u>

- Niche search automation tools - <u>Offervault</u>

Content SEO

1. SEO plugins

- <u>Yoast SEO</u>

- <u>Google Analytics for WordPress</u>

- <u>All-In-One SEO Pack</u>

- <u>Platinum SEO</u>

- <u>Scribe SEO</u>

- <u>Broken Link Checker</u>

- <u>Rel NoFollow Checkbox</u>

- <u>LinkPatrol</u>

2. Non-Plugin SEO tools

- <u>SEMrush</u>

- <u>Google Keyword Planner</u>

- KeywordTool.io

- Open Site Explorer

- Keywords Explorer

- KWfinder

- SERPWatcher

Engagement, Publicity and Promotion

- Disqus plug-in -

- Facebook Comments plugin -

- Twitter Plugins- Better Click To Tweet, TweetDis, Click To Tweet, etc.

- Social Media Share (amalgam) – e.g. AddThis, ShareThis, Social Welfare, etc.

- Email marketing automation tools - Aweber, Mailchimp, Getresponse

Page loading efficiency

The following are tools that can greatly help you boost your page's loading speed;

- Speed diagnostics - Google Page Speed Insights, P3 Plug-in Profiler, Web Page Test, GTmetrix, Pingdom, Load Impact

- Cache plugins – W3 Total Cache, WP Fastest Cache, WP Super Cache, Cache Enabler,

- Minify plugins – WP Super Minify, Better WordPress Minify, WP Smush.it,

- CDNs – CDN Enabler, Cloud flare,

- Lazy Loaders – BJ Lazy Load, Ajax Load More

Administrative plugins

- Akismet

- Bulk Move

- SI CAPCHA Antispam

- WordPress Importer

- WP PageNavi

- Categories Images

- Delete Expired Transients

- Social Networks Auto-Poster (SNAP)

- Posts Date Ranges

- Date Range Filter

- Contact Form 7

- Menu Bar

- Posts by Tag

- Posts in Page

- Posts in Shortcode

- Transients Manager

- WP Optimize

- WP PageNavi

JetPack plug-in suite

JetPack Suite comprises of a package containing several essential tools for your WordPress Blog;

- Site Stats and Analytics

- Automatic Sharing on social networks (Facebook, Twitter, LinkedIn, Tumblr, Reddit, Whatsapp,

- Related Posts

- SEO tools

- Advertising program

- Security and backup

- Content curation

- Discussions and community interactions (in-house)

- Expert support

NOTE:

For purposes of fast performance and non-conflict amongst various plugins, it is important to limit your plugs to only the most essential. As a rule of thumb, you should have no more than 8 plugins. The higher the number of plugins, the higher the risk of conflict and incompatibility with your theme; and also the higher the risk of slow page loading speed. Thus, you must carefully consider trade-offs.

OTHER WAYS TO GENERATE TRAFFIC

There are many ways to generate traffic for your website. So far, we have discussed Organic SEO (use of Keywords). The following are some of the other ways by which you can direct traffic to your blog;

- Paid SEO (PPC)
- Social media PPC
- Email marketing
- Forum discussion
- Commenting on niche-related blogs
- Social media profile
- Youtube video posting
- Documenting and posting interview of an influential blogger
- Guest blogging

Paid SEO

Paid SEO refers to driving traffic to your website by use of Keywords which are paid for. The keywords could be the same organic keywords that we have previously discussed. The only difference is that, you pay a Search Engine provider to rank your web page on SERP based on user queries that relate to your keywords. Thus, the ranking is not organic but advertised.

Social Media PPC

PPC stands for Pay Per Click. This is the most common form of online advertising whereby adverts are strategically placed in user access points to draw their attention. Facebook is the most commonly used Social media for PPC. When you log into Facebook there are certain adverts that appear on the sidebars and sometimes together with feeds. These are PPC adverts.

You can pay Facebook to render such PPC adverts on your behalf.

Email Marketing

Email marketing refers to use of emails to drive traffic to your website. You can create content with targetable links to your web page and send to various email addresses based on potential leads. When the targeted leads get impressed by the content, they click on the links provided within the emailed content which leads them to your web page.

Forum discussion

Forums are a great way to draw traffic to your website. You simply find forums that are relevant to your blog niche and subscribe to them. Afterwards, you can offer relevant advice or opinion on a topical issue and provide your credentials (including your name and website link) so that those who desire more information can access it.

Commenting on niche-related blogs

Just like Forum discussion, make a list of authority blogs relevant to your niche. Offer helpful comments relevant to the topical issue at hand. At the end of the comment, provide your credentials for follow-up (include link to your relevant web page in the link)

Social media profile

Having a social media profile, is a great way to engage your audience. LinkedIn, Google Plus, Facebook and Twitter are great place to derive traffic via your social media profile. The first three are extremely helpful if you are offering professional services (such as content writing, SEO, etc).

Youtube video posting

YouTube has gained reputation of one of the best ways to drive traffic to your site, especially if you are targeting millennials as your audience. Studies have shown that millennials prefer viewing content rather than reading them. The best videos are those 'How to' videos that demonstrate how to use a particular product, how to benefit from certain product features, and so on.

Create a 'How to' video relevant to your blog and link to your blog so that those who want further details can get in touch with your web page.

The great advantage is that, YouTube has provisions to enable you monetize your videos. Thus, if you intend to monetize your blog, then, this is an extra income alternative.

Documenting and posting interview of an influential blogger

Every niche has an influential blogger, that is, a blogger who has a huge loyal following. An influential blogger can help you gain a significant volume of traffic, especially if you are relatively new entrant with quality content and valued service addition. Simply invite an influential blogger to an interview. A video-recorded interview (that you will also transcribe) is the best option. Request the influential blogger to inform his/her audience about the interview and provide links to your website where the interview video and/or verbatim transcription are. This way, the influencer's audience will become aware of your blog and will trust it based on the authority of the influential blogger. In some cases, you might need to pay the influencer for the services of an influencer.

Guest blogging

Guest blogging refers to registering to send posts to authority sites on topical issues that you are expert in. The primary aim of guest blogging is to have an opportunity to expose yourself and your blog and gain valuable backlinks to your blog.

BEST 5 WAYS TO MONETIZE YOUR BLOG

Monetizing your blog is the processes of making your blog earn you some revenue. The following are the 5 best ways to monetize your blog;

1. Affiliate marketing

2. Sale of advertisement space

3. Membership subscription

4. Sale of content materials - eBooks/training manuals, podcasts/ videos

5. Sale of service e.g. through webinars, virtual

Affiliate marketing

Affiliate marketing refers to use of your blog content to market certain products. The following steps will help you to succeed in affiliate marketing;

1. Determine the type of your site

2. Determine the niche products to market

3. Get affiliate links

4. Use affiliate links into your blog

Determine your type of site

The following are the main types of affiliate sites;

- Daily deals

- Price comparisons

- Product review

- "How to" sites

Determine the niche products to market

The products that you have to market must be relevant to your content. Thus, you must find the niche products that best-fits your content. More importantly, if you decide to use your blog for affiliate marketing purposes, then, it is of utmost importance that you find the product niche first prior to writing content about your product niche.

Get Affiliate links

Affiliate links are special links that you can use to hyperlink your content to particular affiliate products that you are marketing.

These are unique links such that they contain a your particular affiliate ID and also the product ID for purposes of monitoring sales made through your affiliate marketing effort.

Use affiliate links into your content to market affiliate products

Once the affiliate network platform gives you affiliate links, you now hyperlink specific content using the links so that readers can possibly click on them to be directed to the affiliate product that you are marketing.

Sale of Advertising Space

The most popular way used by bloggers to monetize their blogs is sale of advertising space.

There are dozens of advertising networks from which you can be able to contact in order for them to post adverts onto your blog. Google Adsense is by far the most popular advertising network program. There are many others.

Membership subscription

Membership subscription is increasingly becoming popular these days as a means of monetizing blogs. If you are offering specialist services such as training, you can create a membership site. In this site, you can sell training materials, webinars, videos, etc.

Membership subscription is the most rewarding way if you do have a highly specialized value-addition service to offer.

Sale of content material

If you have content that you can sell such as eBooks, podcasts, webinars, videos, apps, etc, you can use your blog as an avenue to market them. There are various plugins that enable you to sell downloadable content through your blog.

Sale of service

As we have seen, you can sell service via membership subscription. The other way to sell services is offer advice regarding through a blog post regarding your expertize and provide your contact so that whoever feels that he/she needs further help, or extra service can contact you for the purposes of hiring you to carry out that particular service. It is common to find 'Hire Me' button at the end of a blog. For example, if you are an expert blogger or WordPress Developer, you can explain certain specific areas of how to set up a WordPress blog, or describe a particular solution to a common WordPress challenge. There are those who might not have the requisite skills or time to implement your recommendations. Thus, they will contact you to implement your prescribed solution on their behalf. This way, you are monetizing your blog by selling certain specific service to them.

AUTOMATE YOUR INCOME

As a blogger, there is a limit to how far you can stretch by doing everything by yourself. Your natural limitations may constrain your income streams. Thus, you need helping hands and effective utilization of technology optimize your income flows. Automation is the secret to multiple figures passive income.

As a publisher, the first and foremost thing that you need to automate is your content. You can achieve content automation through the following ways;

- Outsourcing content creation

- Outsourcing content marketing

It is imperative that, as you grow you will need to expand your scope by having more niches. Each niche will require its own website blog. Thus, you will need to create several websites. You can automate blog creation in the following ways;

- Outsourcing web development

- Outsourcing niche domain research

With content automation and web development automation, the capacity become large such that you need to have your affiliate links strategically placed on your blogs. To achieve this you will need;

- Virtual assistants

- Virtual administrator (in case you employ several virtual assistants)

To optimize your content and blog structure for search engines, you will need an SEO expert who will assess and evaluate the performance of your blogs on various search engines and perform the necessary tweaks to achieve optimal performance.

There are several freelancing sites where you can easily hire affordable virtual assistants and virtual administrators and other freelance technical staff. Popular among these freelancing sites include;

- Upwork

- Freelancer

- Fiverr

Automating tools

There are many automation tools available that you can use to improve automation of your income. The good thing is that WordPress has many automation tools availed as plugins. Choosing WordPress as your CMS can greatly boost your automation effort.

The following are the main categories of automation tools;

- Niche search automation tools

- Content marketing automation tools

- Web development automation tools

- Social media automation tools

- Email automation tools

- SEO tools

- Traffic performance monitoring tools

We have already discussed most of these tools in the Section titled "Other SEO Add-Ins /Software". However, we can give a brief description of each of these categories that haven't been covered in the previous sections.

Niche search automation tools

These are tools that make it easy to find profitable affiliate niches.

Content marketing automation tools

Content marketing automation tools are tools that enable you to easily market your content in the most optimal way. These include Forum boards, demonstration videos (YouTube) – review, instructions, applications, special features, etc, landing page creation tools, among others.

Web development automation tools

These are tools that enable you to automate creation of websites. There are several such tools including Wix among others. However, in this case, we focus on those that help you automate creation of WordPress blogs. These include;

- Softaculous – this is the most widely used automation tool for creating WordPress blogs. It is a free tool installed by most hosts who offer CPanel for managing your host.

Other than these tools, there are those specialized WordPress host providers whom you can instruct to create WordPress websites for you at some extra fee.

Social media marketing automation tools

Social media marketing tools enables you to post content on various social networks in the most optimized way. There are many such tools. Other than these general tools, each social network has its own unique tools that enable you to post directly from your website into your social network page or timeline.

To get each of these plugins, access the developer section of each of these social networks right from within your account.

Email marketing automation tools

When you have hundreds of email contacts to deal with, it becomes a tough task to post to them and promptly respond to feedback. Thus, there are various auto-responders (email posting and responding tools) that are available to enable you automate this task. The following are some of the most popular email marketing automation tools.

SEO tools

See section titled Other SEO Add-Ins / Software to Use

Traffic performance monitoring tools

See section titled Other SEO Add-Ins / Software to Use

CONCLUSION

Thank you for acquiring this book and being with us in reading through it all.

It is my sincere hope that you have gained valuable lessons and gotten inspired to start a blog or optimize your already existing blog for SEO. It is also my sincere hope that you have been able to share knowledge and information with others regarding what you have learned and how they can be able to acquire this book and keep it as a point of reference and wealth of knowledge in their store.

Again, thank for acquiring this book!